Building Character

Showing Perseverance

by Rebecca Pettiford

Bullfrog Books

Ideas for Parents and Teachers

Bullfrog Books let children practice reading informational text at the earliest reading levels. Repetition, familiar words, and photo labels support early readers.

Before Reading

- Discuss the cover photo. What does it tell them?

- Look at the picture glossary together. Read and discuss the words.

Read the Book

- "Walk" through the book and look at the photos. Let the child ask questions. Point out the photo labels.

- Read the book to the child, or have him or her read independently.

After Reading

- Prompt the child to think more. Ask: How do you show perseverance? How do you feel when you persevere?

Bullfrog Books are published by Jump!
5357 Penn Avenue South
Minneapolis, MN 55419
www.jumplibrary.com

Library of Congress Cataloging-in-Publication Data

Names: Pettiford, Rebecca, author.
Title: Showing perseverance / by Rebecca Pettiford.
Description: Minneapolis, Minnesota: Jump!, Inc., 2018. | Series: Building character | "Bullfrog Books are published by Jump!" | Includes index.
Audience: Ages 5–8. | Audience: K to Grade 3.
Identifiers: LCCN 2017030348 (print)
LCCN 2017030608 (ebook)
ISBN 9781624966484 (ebook)
ISBN 9781620318881 (hardcover: alk. paper)
ISBN 9781620318898 (pbk.)
Subjects: LCSH: Perseverance (Ethics)—Juvenile literature.
Classification: LCC BJ1533.P4 (ebook)
LCC BJ1533.P4 P48 2017 (print) | DDC 179/.9—dc23
LC record available at https://lccn.loc.gov/2017030348

Editor: Kirsten Chang
Book Designer: Michelle Sonnek
Photo Researchers: Michelle Sonnek & Kirsten Chang

Photo Credits: Guas/Shutterstock, cover (medal); Ljupco Smokovski/Shutterstock, cover (boy); shapecharge/iStock, 1; Sergey Novikov/Shutterstock, 3; Vaclav Volrab/Shutterstock, 4, 23tl; Anna Nahabed/Shutterstock, 5, 23tr; asiseeit/iStock, 6–7; gjohnstonphoto/iStock, 8, 23bl; Lykovata/Shutterstock, 9; KK Tan/Shutterstock, 10–11; wavebreakmedia/Shutterstock, 12–13, 23br; Ty Allison/Getty, 14; Jim Barber/Shutterstock, 15; Mat Hayward/Shutterstock, 16–17; Andreas P/Adobe Stock, 18–19, 20–21; panphai/Adobe Stock, 22; all_about_people/Shutterstock, 24.

Printed in the United States of America at Corporate Graphics in North Mankato, Minnesota.

Table of Contents

We Can Do It!

Life gives us challenges.

It may be hard.

But we do not give up.

We keep going.

We show perseverance.

It takes time to do your best.

It takes hard work.

Will juggles.

Oops! A ball falls.

It is OK. He keeps trying.

Kat plays piano.

She sets a goal.

She practices every day.

She learns a new song!

tutor

Reading is hard
for Eric.

A tutor helps him.

Now he loves
to read.

Kay runs a race.

Oh, no!

It looks like she will not win.

But she finishes the race.

She does not give up.

Mark misses the shot.

He keeps trying.

He knows he will
get better.

Climbing is hard.
We go one step
at a time.

We did it!

How to Juggle

Learning a new skill or activity takes time. It takes perseverance. You have to keep trying, even if it is hard. In this activity, you will learn how to juggle.

Directions:

1. Get two tennis balls. Practice throwing one ball in an arc like a rainbow, from one hand to the other. Keep your hands at waist level. Throw no higher than eye level.
2. Now throw the ball back in an arc to the other hand. Keep doing this until you are good at it. You will probably drop the ball a few times. Do not give up. Keep trying!
3. Pick up a second ball. Hold one ball in each hand.
4. If you are right handed, start the first throw from your right hand. Wait less than a second.
5. Now throw the second ball from your left hand before you catch the first ball with your left hand. Then catch the second ball in your right hand.
6. Keep practicing!

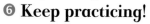

Picture Glossary

challenges
Things that
are hard to do.

perseverance
To keep doing
something in spite
of difficulties,
challenges,
or hardship.

juggles
Keeps several
objects moving
in the air at
the same time.

tutor
A teacher who
works with
one student.

Index

To Learn More

Learning more is as easy as 1, 2, 3.

1) Go to www.factsurfer.com

2) Enter "showingperseverance" into the search box.

3) Click the "Surf" button to see a list of websites.

With factsurfer.com, finding more information is just a click away.

24